Tesoro

Yesika Salyado

Salgado, Yesika

1st edition

ISBN: 978-1-945649-23-3

Edited by Safia Elhillo
Proofread by Rhiannon McGavin
Cover design by Cassidy Trier
Editorial design by Ian DeLucca

Not a Cult
Los Angeles, CA

for
Saya and Henry
my two lemon trees

Contents

III.

IV.

V.

Corazón,

months ago when I began conceptualizing this book I
thought it would be this grand bilingual story about my
family. I imagined myself interviewing my mother, tías
and primas. I wanted to gather our history of survival. I
wanted to do it in both of my languages. as I wrote and
searched my archives for poems, the story began to slowly
change. ripen. I began answering questions I have asked
before but the answers were clear now. how did I learn
to love? to forgive? how did I become the woman, lover
and poet that I am? this book turned into a closer look
at myself. all the women I have been, who I will be. my
hunger for answers. the gray space between my languages.
the balance of two countries. the city I was born into. the
bitter and sweet of my life. Tesoro is the unearthing of
what is most sacred to me. my treasure; the women who
raised me, the women who keep me, the woman that I
am. I hope you see yourself in them. I hope they coax the
bittersweet out of you too.

yours,
Yesika

I.

I come from women
who fend for themselves

Nostalgia

there are two lemon trees in our garden. small dusty seeds
that were planted before we moved in twenty nine years
ago. every spring they grow heavy with fruit. sometimes
I stand barefoot between them. my big toe nudging their
children rotting on the floor. the neighbors come with
bags to carry away the living. take as many as you want I
say as I shut the door. I do not wonder what becomes of
them. if they go on to be sweet or bitter or both. inside, I
write a love note to a mango hanging on a tree I have not
seen in years.

Canela

I am a brown woman who writes poetry about her brown
life. I read it out loud and my accent curls the corners
of my words. I am made of two languages coiled into the
braid of my tongue. I belong to this country and to the
one who birthed my mother. I write the coffee-stained
edges of my world. the soft caramel of my grandmother.
the hazelnut of my sisters. the cinnamon skin of the man
I love. I am built of colors. I have named them holy and
they each bring the poems to me. look at the cursive of my
flesh. it is how the stories arrive. it is how they leave. with
me. intact. inseparable. complete.

The Women

where do I begin?
mami?
my tías?
my grandmother?

do I follow the bruises to El Salvador?
do I dissect each fist here in Los Angeles?

I am a freight train with no conductor
all I know is the blow of my whistle

a single question:

how did you survive the men?

Polaroid

my favorite photograph of my mother / her red dress /
her long curls over one shoulder / her hands / small ships
taking port on her lap / the couch / a land she calls hers
/ she smiles without parting her lips / her night sky eyes
staring into the lens

my favorite photograph of my parents / they dance
together / my mother and her red dress / her hand curled
around my father's shoulder / her bare arms / a new gold
/ my father's thick hair / a black cloud above them / he
smiles / my mother does not / she stares into the camera
again

my favorite photograph of myself / my parents sit on
the sand / Santa Monica Beach / the cars in the distance
catch the sun in their metal / my parents are kissing / my
mother's legs shaped into a question mark / my father's
mustache / a stroke of danger / and there / in their eyes / a
twinkle / me

Terremotos

y

they lived in a tiny house
with missing windows
so it always seemed
as if their home was squinting

its front yard
a tangled mess of balding hair
rusty lawn furniture,
old bicycles and two lemon trees

the kitchen's linoleum
sang beneath
the mother's shifting weight
as she washed dishes before bed

the father,
read his newspaper in the dining room
a bottle of vodka hidden beneath his chair
the radio tuned to
sad, slow
honey thick
boleros
spread
evenly over the dinner table

in the bedroom
the three sisters
wild even when silent

their books, poems
and drawings covered
every surface of the house

there were pets
sometimes a dog
sometimes a cat
sometimes a rabbit
or turtle
or pigeon
once for an hour
a baby possum
until the mother
made the second daughter
give it back

at nights
the tiny house
became a jail cell
with shouting matches
and riots
everyone
pushed and pushed
until the walls
threatened to burst

but never did

the mother
would return
to the kitchen
the father
would leave
in search of more drink
and the three sisters
would
laugh

loud
over the music
over the hurt
everyone fought over
but never spoke about
they would howl
their best wild howls
and the mother would threaten
to come out of the kitchen with a sandal
the father would sigh
calling them
terremotos

and they were

in that tiny house
they shook so good
you couldn't tell
if things were the way they were
from disaster
or because
they liked it
that way

Mami's Cooking

Mami says that every house should always have a pot of
frijoles. Mami says that good pupusas aren't only about
the ingredients but also about how round they are. that
every cup of coffee needs pan dulce. an egg, queso fresco
and a tortilla can be a meal. the chicken needs more
tomato sauce. she needs to bake something to warm up
the house. banana bread because the bananas are going
bad. keeps the stale rolls in the freezer to make bread
pudding later. Mami says the cousins are coming over and
need feeding. the neighbor brought over carne asada and
she has to cook something to return with their plate. asks
if I am ready for dinner. says try this. take a little bite. I put
some away for you. Mami and her small kitchen. the rattle
of her dishes. her heavy pans. her smile as we eat and say
que rico. her dancing eyes when we ask for more. Mami
and the way she feeds us her neverending heart. *come taste
this. I saved you some. do you want me to pour it into a bowl? I
was waiting for you.*

Excuses

o

my father's father killed himself
and my father was only a child

when he found him hanging
from a mango tree

my great grandmother tried to love
the death out of him
but he was a man, and you know how men are.
he started drinking more and more
then the civil war struck El Salvador like lightning
and he was tortured by soldiers
he never told me but I saw the scars
saw him crying to himself
I would ask what was wrong
and he would say
I didn't deserve to know

and this is manhood, isn't it?

and being a woman
is being an apology, right?
isn't it being the other cheek?
my mother is a saint

she is rushing home at six o'clock
because her husband needs dinner

she is tears over the sink
and a tender goodnight

she is the girl three different men
tried to push themselves onto
they couldn't help but want to take

didn't need to ask because her beauty
was all the yes they needed

my father was one of these men
took her to a hotel room

told her, *you are not leaving here
without being mine*
then she was his because
she figured it was time she belonged to a man
nine months later there I was
and I am hers

didn't it all work out?

In Our Family

u

in our family the husbands die on you early
and old age is spent
in churches or
with daughters
raising children
you are too tired
to love properly

you get phone calls on weekends
letters only the first Saturday of the month
visits yearly

everyone comes
with their noise and suitcases
their English that sounds as if
they were speaking
from beneath the ocean

your grandchildren forget their Spanish
speak it gargled and backwards
they hate the insects
the sun
the food
complain of boredom
claim all of the hammocks
almost kill the dogs and chickens
from the fright of their fireworks
lose your good pots down by the river
spread themselves all over the compound
they put out the candles on your altar,
hide your statue of the Virgin Mary in their bedsheets
refuse to pray the rosary with you
and are surprised when you come after them with a fly swatter
when you ask your daughter not to bring them next time

in our family the word *grandmother* is holy
and never said in vain
she is spoken of in reverence
and the younger generations
question her as if she were theology

calling cards become tickets to confessionals
all the children and their children
dialing the long numbers
to hear her voice
unfold itself like
dusty polaroids
kept wrapped in worn handkerchiefs
yellowed reminders
of where you came from
of where you've been
of what you are

in our family,
grandmothers are God
you come to them with hands extended
thankful and in awe
they survive all
become the only constant
the compass of our entire tribe

the men, they all die early

but God
sweeps up her porch
coils the long braid of her hair
into a knot held
at the nape of her neck

and stretches her arms wide
when everyone comes
home
one more time

Tamales

Mami. Tía Marina. Tía Reina. Tía Paz. Tía Morena. Tías
with names forgotten. borrowed Tías. adopted Tías.
cousins old enough to be Tías. all busy at the table.

I am a little girl with her curls pulled into bun. today I
get to hold a ladle and scoop the masa onto the banana
leaves. I pass it along to a Tía who adds the salsa. another
adds chicken. another potato. another ejote. another
wraps it and drops it into a pot the size of my body. Mami
makes a joke. *if no one brings presents we have plenty tamales
to unwrap at midnight.* everyone laughs at the same joke we
hear every Christmas. the Tías gossip and I pretend not
to listen. I watch as they laugh, stir pots and smooth their
hands over their aprons. my sisters call my name. I ignore
them. I am learning magic today.

Las Locas

the tía that threatened to jump off the fire escape if her
husband left to the bar
the one who chased her husband around the lemon trees
with a frying pan
the one who pretends to faint whenever she needs her
sons to stay
the one who drinks beer and plays poker
the one who had an affair
the prima who let the ex husband keep the children
the prima who has taken too many husbands to count
the one who joined the army and left for years
the one who doesn't show up for family parties
the one who talks about dating women without hesitation
the childless one who drinks margaritas on mondays
the one that asks her mother if she regrets not having
more lovers
the one who lives out of her suitcase
who doesn't cook or clean, who forgets to call,
who wears red lipstick and sheer shirts to thanksgiving
dinner
the chismosa no one tells scandals to
because she writes everything down
tell me about that time again
where you were free,
when you made a mess,
and were forgiven
the way we forgive the men

II.

before I knew
what I know now
before these
palm trees
loved me
back

1995

the summer I spent in Gainesville / long before love asked
for my skin / when the blood came for the first time /
while mami was thousands of miles away / I was learning
to swim / trusting the water with my body / my uncle
didn't think I was doing it quickly enough / grabbed my
life vest / took me far out into the lake / *swim back* / but I
just floated there / crying / until my cousin / came / took
my hand / led me back / where my toes touched sand / to
this day / I still don't know how / to swim

First Kiss

we were standing between the lemon trees / 16 years old
/ he said that girls with feathered bangs drove him crazy /
my curls had no bangs / if they did they wouldn't feather /
like the pretty cholas / I smiled / but it wasn't a real smile /
more like something to fill the space between us / he said
he liked me because I was nice to him / I felt something
in my stomach / nothing like butterflies / they lied / it was
painful / he asked if he could kiss me / I wanted to run
and hide / I wanted to unzip my skin and let him wear it /
he said my friends were pretty but I was funny / I nodded
/ I knew I couldn't be both / we kissed / but / whenever he
touched my hair / I remembered / I stopped telling jokes
/ nice girls rot like this / nice girls aren't always nice / I
learned / eventually

Thanksgiving
a

don't touch your chiches too much or they'll get all saggy
Tía Marina scolded me when I was fifteen
marveling over my growing body

you can tell when a girl has lost her virginity.
she gets hips, ass, her body turns into a woman.
Tío Alirio leans across the table to Silvana,

have you had sex yet?

when the first boy and I
lay naked on his parents' bed
his face soft and flushed over mine
when he found his way into me
and my heart wasn't where I kept it anymore
but instead on the ceiling, the wall,
the window facing the busy street
I was a sudden gasp and he a shattering of flesh

I dressed, snuck into my home
washed my face and hands,
joined my family for thanksgiving dinner
I held my breath as my uncle
looked at me from across the table
I wondered if I had already changed
if he'd ring the alarm and give me away
but everything went on the same.
I smiled,
pretending to be a girl
that wants to know nothing
about her womanhood

Phone Sex

r

the first time a man said *I love you* / I had never seen his
face / it came between
grunts / questions of underwear / and how hard I could
take it / I was a child
and had found the number in a phone book / somewhere
I could call / and / someone would
always listen / to the sound of my voice / the shallow of
my breath / turning me into / a cliff
they were begging to jump off

when my mother / blocked the numbers / I told her were
psychic hotlines / I then found the internet / full of men /
trembling to touch / the small of my prepubescent back / I
was good at saying
the best things / words had always been my best toys / I
shared them willingly

when I got older / a flesh and bone boy climbed over my
body / I closed my eyes tight
pretending his mouth / was a phone receiver / and / I
was nothing but a stream of of words / climbing out of
places / I kept hidden / from my parents / my priest / my
conscience / my god

this boy working away at me / digging into me / like those
phone men / trembling to slide themselves in / didn't
know how long I'd been waiting to hear / *I love you* / from
someone who sees my face / someone who drinks from it /
as if it were all there was / for their parched lips

that I'd been waiting / to have someone steal the knot
in my throat / take it as their own / far far away from the
night / I found a number in a phone book and let men /
rub themselves raw as they listened / to the poetry I had
yet to learn / a blessing
and never a curse

San Vicente, El Salvador
e

I lay
a starfish girl
on the bed of a pickup truck
the sky
a candy blue
as we drive up
the road
cutting like
a party ribbon
around a volcano
another truck
bigger and dustier
than ours roars by
it is heavy with men
covered in ash and sweat
I know by their tired faces
they've been working
the cotton or sugar fields all day
they are headed home
to warm tortillas and frijoles

maybe if it's a good day
una sopa de pollo

San Vicente
is church bells
and a cathedral
I can see for miles

the sun is setting
the sky a watercolor painting

I sit up and my hair
becomes a waving flag

we drive in and out
of small towns and villages
each a knot of noise, of color, smells
each a rosary bead
each a pebble leading us home

I am
only eyes
no mouth
no hands
I give my heart
to the horizon
this is my land
I was made of this dirt

San Vicente a speck behinds us
I am a starfish girl again
the stars are out and waving back at me

I pray we never stop driving
but the road becomes familiar
I hear my uncle and mother laughing
from inside the truck's cabin
as we slow

I sit up again
for a second there
I was all Salvadoran
the sky, volcano and road agreed

No Language

tell him you're a Mexican

nah I'm Salvi,
I don't look up from my plate
when the school bell rings

va pues cerota, vámonos
their laughter cracks the sky in two

I let the stream of students
move my body
to my Honors English class

I sit at the desk nearest to the door
teacher calls on me to read
stops me mid sentence
enunciate please

the sky in my mouth leaves the room

The Pretty Girl

Tupac is playing loud
and we are all singing along
I take a slow drag from the joint,
someone makes a joke of it
I am the nerd that knows all the words to the song
who would have known?
we are parked somewhere in Echo Park
the sun is making golden cheekbones of us
my parents think I am at school
but here I am inhaling a poem
about brown boys and the way their eyes soften
when Liliana walks out of her house
her long dark hair a veil caught in the wind
she climbs into the back seat with me
takes the joint from my hands
laughs like she is the only reason
anyone could ever smile
and we all agree

Panic

crying while putting on socks / thinking of skipping
school / thinking of sleeping all day / panic comes / not
a wave / more earthquake / jammed door way / can't get
out / can't even stand / think of calling out of work / guilt
/ broken / you / why are you like this?/ why aren't you
normal? / more crying / bed is not bed / more a temporary
death / alive so exhausting / rather not move / until you're
less / you / *no one talk to me* / thinking of missing work /
wash face / get bag / deep breath / sit on couch too long /
cry more / quiet now / quiet / time to go / will they know?
/ you survived?

Echo Park

on Saturdays we used to hop on the 4 headed downtown.
we'd jump out at Echo Park Blvd. first, we'd hit up
Fashion Forever where they sold the stretchy jeans that
forgave my panza. they never lasted very long but they
did the trick. one time we had a few extra dollars and
my white eyeliner looked pretty dope. my best friend's
baby oiled hair caught the light just right. we took some
glamour shot pictures. we argued over the background.
I wanted pink hearts, she insisted on green stars. she
won. we got hungry and hunted down an elotero. this
was a long time ago. like, before they re-did the lake. back
when no one touched the water. half outta respect and
half outta fear. they found a dead body once, I heard.
you don't mess with that. I used to dream about taking
my Quinceañera pictures with the red bridge and palm
trees behind me. now, you can't take a picture without
someone showing up in the background. doing couples
yoga or tight rope walking between the trees, you know,
weird white people shit. all you want is the water and the
downtown skyline behind you. like back then when you
took photos and prayed they developed good enough to
keep. sometimes they'd be blank or your thumb would
creep into a corner like a pink sun. shit ain't like that
anymore. I take my niece to the park and pray there are
some brown kids for her to run around with. I search
for the mothers that look like the women in my family. I
sit nearby. listen to them talk amongst themselves. I type
away into my phone. it's the only way home nowadays.

Pacoima

the valley / Marco, Xochi, Rose / their parents / their
house / the pool / the dogs / Marco's car / Kanye's College
Dropout / Jesus Walks / hot nights outside of In and
Out / hot nights at Venice Beach / hot nights at Placerita
Canyon / the smell of weed / the beer / liquor / Khurby's
pick up truck / Vicente Fernandez / ten of us in an air
conditioned bedroom / Xochi and I the only girls / so
much talking / laughing / sleepover / like this / like 7am
would always be our bedtime / like we'd be dancing on
beaches until sunrise all our lives / like dinner from Little
Caesars would never get old / like every house party was
waiting for us to crash it / Marco was a brown boy so
brown they called him black / his parents Salvadoran
/ before I knew words like diaspora and Afro-Latino /
when I didn't understand / why my loving him made my
parents uncomfortable / when the homies called him the
n word / a joke / they said / and I lectured everyone until
they rolled their eyes / Pacoima / so long ago / we drove
up the canyon one day / the car stalled on the way back
down / 5am / Khurby put the car on cruise control / Marco
and Xochi / twin brother and sister / sat on the moon
roof / I held their legs / we flew down into the city lights
/ the homie Dizzy on the hood of the car / we / Central
American and young / free as fuck / laughter and wind in
our lungs / the canyon caught fire a year or two later / we
never went back / Marco met someone / three children / I
fell in love with someone else / my father died / the world
ended / slowly / like another life I once lived / Pacoima / I
say / like I was never there

La Americana

the year the big earthquake happened in El Salvador
/ Jenny and I went anyway / a month later / a second
earthquake / mami called us / her voice another tremor
/ we were fine / I was trying to forget / my first love /
hoping he'd shake loose / I wanted to leave him / on the
side of the road / wanted to wash him off / in a river / my
grandmother / would laugh at my sadness / what did I
know of love? / I couldn't wash my own calzones / didn't
know how to palmear any tortillas / I burned the rice / if
she had raised me / I would be more stone than pulp / a
good girl / that goes to church / prays her rosary / keeps
her mouth shut / instead / I am a huevona with poems /
mamá deje a la niña / Tía Marina would say / she'd bring
me a warm tortilla con requeson / *toma* / she played Juan
Gabriel softly before bed / her way of telling me / *go ahead
and cry* / when it was time to return to mami / Tía packed
my broken heart back into my luggage / wrapped it in
newspaper / tucked it between / the hocote preserves and
dried cheese / *put it to use* / she said / and I did

III.

you loved me so much
it feels like you didn't love me at all

Sweetheart

my teeth ache
at the sound
of your name

Bittersweet

the one time you visited my home
I asked you to wait outside
between the lemon trees

I caught a quick glimpse of
a six foot tall, moonlit you
through the kitchen window
rooting yourself into my limbs

I stepped back out
shutting the door
to the chatter of my family
let's go, I'm ready

what would our story be
if I had asked you to come inside?
if you had taken a seat on the couch
across from my mother
your halted Spanish
cómo está?
your dark brown hand in mine

mami, él es mi novio

her timid English
welcome
asking you to stay

Tonsillectomy

t

I don't think you ever loved me, you say

I think of my throat surgery. how I was awake on a
hospital bed and then I wasn't. hours later someone kept
saying my name. I was so far away and didn't want to
come back. I woke up to my doctor calling my name. I
couldn't speak. I was moved to a new room. tubes down
my throat. nurses would talk to me and all I could do was
nod. got sent home the next day. couldn't eat anything
solid for weeks. lived off ice cream, jello and chocolate
pudding. one afternoon my sisters baked a pizza. I had
never wanted something so bad that it hurt. I snuck into
the kitchen. tore off a piece. slipped it in my mouth. let
it sit on my tongue until it became mush. spit it out. I
cried for hours afterwards. I could smell it through my
bedroom door. when I healed, my voice changed. a small
smooth pebble I slid through my teeth. you called and
thought you had dialed the wrong number. I laughed. *it's
me.*
you were what I had been waiting to eat. what I hoped
would heal.

I do. I do love you. I spit you out into the sink, cried myself
to sleep.

Tamarindo

I text
good morning
but meant to type
why are we not waking up in the same bed?

Bipolar

car ride home / I tell you when I was young / I got
diagnosed with bipolar II / I romanticized being crazy
/ a woman with a beehive for a head / your mother was
bipolar too / I ask if you love her / you don't say anything
/ there is an accident on the freeway and traffic is at a
standstill / I take your hand into both of mine / ask if
you've ever imagined your funeral / you shrug / I ask more
about your mother / you sigh / I tell you about my father /
his belt / his drinking / his anger / you squeeze my hand /
I laugh / I've learned to laugh at my darkness / the traffic
moves / you exit the highway and pull up to my home / I
kiss you / a long winding kiss / I say goodbye /
our love eventually runs out / I don't imagine my funeral
anymore /
I do imagine you coming back / the illness changes its
name

She Names You Corazón

corazón, she says in the same voice she says your name.
you know some Spanish. mostly things your grandmother
said to the tv. your girlfriend speaks so much Spanish
your head spins. when she's with her family she switches
languages so quickly you get whiplash. she's always asking
questions about your life. *how many cousins do you have?*
which one is your best friend? who's your favorite aunt? do you
call your family in Puerto Rico? where did your parents meet?
did your mother teach your father any Spanish? you know,
back in El Salvador... is how she starts half her stories.
they're usually about her abuela she keeps forgetting is
dead now. about the moon being a real moon there. not
this soft bulb here. says she experiences everything twice,
even love. first in one language then another. you forget
which one comes first. when you make love you search
for words you haven't said since childhood. your tongue
a hook in shallow water. hardly anything surfaces but
you try. *corazón, I love you.* she says. you believe her. you
wonder what stories of you she tells to her family. she
stretches her arm against yours. *look baby, cafe con leche.*
laughs and presses her mouth to your chest. you don't
know if she is talking to you or your heart. months later
you break up. suddenly El Salvador is everywhere. a lady
selling sweet bread on the subway calls you corazón and
the world goes grey for a second. you call her when you
get home. she doesn't answer. she's gone.

Amargura
h

you asked me once
lips wedged between mine,
hands knuckle-deep into curls,
bedsheets cocooning
our bodies; would you be
welcomed into this bed
once married?

the answer came
a suicide yes
a Mary Magdalene promise

the sex never worth the truth
but my hands caved
with too much air between us

you asked
and I gave

a white flag

my hair washing your feet

a pact made with the next woman
the future wife you knew would come
even as you pulled my hips closer:

take him
I've kept his bones warm
just for you

The Belly Has Questions

what if I got in the way?
was he embarrassed?
did he wish I'd disappear?
does the new woman have one?
was I why he left?
others have loved me, why not him?
remember the man who kissed me?
called me beautiful?
why didn't he?
why couldn't he?

Scandal

I should have yelled. smashed a glass on the floor. flipped
a table. swept all the picture frames from the mantle. I
should have roared. let the hairs on the back of my neck
stand straight. should have hissed. held my nails to your
throat. I should have made the neighbors come running.
have them pounding at your door. have them drag me out
by my feet. as I pointed one finger straight at you. cursed
you. swore I'd be back. swore I'd make you pay. instead.
I left quiet while you slept. her name and text message
glowing on your screen. *I love you baby.* I slipped out. my
tears trailing behind. breadcrumbs I knew I'd someday
follow back. the moon shaking her head at my cowardice.
I should have listened to her. I should have howled.
brought sirens. turned the night to a scandal. my heart
on the roof. ready to jump. the crowd forms. the police
asking *what happened?* the text message a flash across the
sky. *I love you baby.* a scene made for a novela. afterwards.
all your life. you'd shiver at the sound of my name. afraid.
this bitch that broke it all. I should have. oh, I should have
taken it all with me.

Forgetting You

the husband with two kids
the weed man with no name
the Colombian with sweet Spanish
the single father with a soft chuckle
the rapper I almost moved in with
the poet with a secret fiancée
the artist with the dog I imagined mine
the lover with a smile like a fishhook
all of them
roads I took
hoping to travel
far away from you.
none of them
got me anywhere
that didn't flood
with the sound of your voice.

How I Know I Haven't Stopped Loving You

you tell a joke
and I laugh so hard
it sounds like
thank God you're back

Sal y Limón

bartender slides a shot over to me / I rub a slice of lemon
on the back of my hand / sprinkle salt / lick it all off / toss
the alcohol down my throat / place the lemon to my lips
and suck / I turn around / smile at Zoe / nod when she
asks if we should dance / I try not to look at you / at the
end of the bar / my old heart / I pretend I don't know
what the room already does / we aren't here together / you
and I / aren't here at all

X

I still don't know
how to look at your skin
without thinking
I've been there before

On Loving Someone That Doesn't Love You Back
e

a dress sits in a window display
you stare so long
you can imagine wearing it
down the street

you gather
all your money
to purchase it

the cashier
asks for
your eyes
instead

Credit

ain't I just a bitter girl that stopped living after you left?
ain't I just a sad thing, over there? ain't all these poems
about you? ain't everything about you? everytime I get
asked why I write, I should just say your name, right? any
article about me just titled "The Woman He Didn't Want
Anymore." my book should have your name on every page.
you made me famous, didn't you? made me so broken
I look like more than what I am. gave me something to
tell all the lonely girls. a violin to play them all to sleep.
you get all the credit. the glory. you get to tell that story. I
loved you and you didn't love me back.

but I told you the night you asked me to stop writing
about you

every poem I have ever written is about me

IV.

*name the nostalgia something sweet
a ripened fruit growing from a dying tree*

The Funeral
s

mami comes home
from El Salvador.
this time she left
to bury her mother.
she asks if we want to see
the video of the funeral.
I don't want to
but nod.
I see all the faces
I know from distance.
the names that can only
be pronounced in Spanish.
the characters in all the stories
mami ever told us.
there is a mariachi singing
women with rosary beads and wet eyes
men in buttoned shirts with sweat stains under their
arms.

the camera focuses on the coffin
and I can see my tiny grandmother
bones and ashen skin
laying among roses and wildflowers

I don't want to look but I do

mami is standing next to the coffin
someone I don't recognize patting her shoulder.
my hands on my lap squeeze each other.

I look across the room

mami sitting on the couch
and she's not crying anymore

this time it is me
with the wet eyes

this is how it is when home
is too far away

and grief comes delayed
in phone calls or videos

we don't know what to do
with our hands
that cannot spread
over the distance and time

the video ends

that night I dream
about the funeral but
this time it is my father's

I am not there again

I wake up to empty hands

always, these empty hands.

St. Patrick's Day
w

eight years ago on a Tuesday
your father and all his body parts
slowed down until
the alcohol finally took
what doctors said
was leaving years ago

you, your mother, and sisters
do what you do best,
you take care of it

plan the wake. call family.
make jokes. feed guests.

tonight
your lover calls after a night of drinking
you tell him you're celebrating
an anniversary you almost forgot

but thank goodness your mother
lit a candle on the dining room table
next to your father's favorite picture of himself
your father's grave is in El Salvador
and this lets you feel like he's less dead

your lover asks if you're okay
you press your back to the mattress

sorry, I guess life is really good now
though you don't know who you are apologizing to

56

Papi's Second Death

my mother's mother leans in
your father was a terrible man
your mother deserved so much more
I slide my headphones on
cry with no sound

my mother's sister tells me
about my father groping her
and I do not want to listen

I know his sins
I lived them

I know his love
I lived it

I grieve for the daughter I will never be again

Tesoro

e

cuando Papi murió
mami took all of his gold and tucked it into her closet
yo me quede con un anillo
he bought me for my quinceañera
no me lo pongo
it's heavy, no me queda
it's always been more his than mine

mamita,
also had gold wrapped in a handkerchief
mami lo guarda en su ropero
back in el Salvador
las argollas, los aretes, las cadenas
she brags about it to other relatives
ella lo heredo por ser la preferida

too many of my stories
empiezan con muerte
I write best when I write from grief
por lo que e perdido
what I am terrified of forgetting
lo que se fue
what haunts me
lo que me queda
treasures I wrap away

tengo ocho años de no ir al Salvador
I've been told it is too dangerous now
y ya no me acuerdo de las milpas
I can't taste the mangoes anymore
o del mar
or the dirt beneath my toes
y tal vez ya no soy de allá

maybe now I'm all american
pero yo nunca quise eso
is this how it that works?
la colonization,
gentrification
vienen aunque nadie las quiera
how do I resist being taken?
como le hago para sentirme
less lost?
a quien le cuento de La Mara Salvatrucha
and the airplanes with tiny seats
de mi español tartamudeado
my fear of flying, hair products in my suitcase
y mi Inglés que no tiene
periods or commas
y los libros
I can only read in English
porque el Español
takes too much work

me pregunta mi amigo
were you born in El Salvador?
y le digo que no
he says, *then you are an American*
y le digo que no
I write this half in Spanish
mitad en Inglés
to show him I'm not really
una americana
or completely anything at all

pero mi Inglés siempre a sido
lo mas bonito que e tenido
mira mi niña
papi would say
good English, so good

y yo sonreía porque
logre ser linda, aunque sea por un ratito

but what was I washing out of my mouth?

mami keeps all my baby teeth in a small jar tucked in
her closet. same place she keeps my father's gold. my
grandmother's jewelry. everything I grew inside me when
my only language was Spanish. what I spit out because I
was told to. told something new was coming. something
permanent. more me. but my teeth are still there. shake
the jar and they will rattle. if you love me, even a little, I
will call you corazón. small and pretty. like the first tooth
my father pulled out of me. look at it. aqui esta. es mio. yo
lo creci. aqui dentro de mi.

remind me again, in what language did I begin telling you
this story?

Bakersfield

e

a truck with an american flag waving behind
we, five Latinas at a table
I ask the women if they are in love
they all say yes
the truck comes around again
we all look
shake our heads and laugh
I pick up my phone
a missed call from my sometimes lover
the night is cold
I am told this town is republican

why my bones
don't feel like my own
tonight

Survival Tactics

t

white man on the dating app
asks why I don't date white men
he likes curvy Latinas
always wanted to sleep with someone like me
he says I'm the smart kind of "Mexican"
the kind with a job and no kids
I probably have a temper
he finds angry women sexy

white man offers to buy me
tickets to any concert
says he can spoil a little brown girl like me
he's already dreaming about it
how holy that would be
how saved I will become

white man is already colonizing
teaching me he is God,
I don't know better
it's his job to show me
after all I am brown
meant to be walked on
like soil
hands
backs

I don't say anything
I don't know who he is
I am only a picture on a website
only a name on a direct message
a profile description that says I am Salvadoran
and only date men of color

meaning,
I can only love you
to find breath in someone
that understands the suffocation
meaning, I can only love somebody
that doesn't look like
what took everything
meaning,
I am only willing to love
my reflection

white man thinks he is the exception

of course he does,
he is a white man
after all

The Therapist
e

I asked my therapist if everyone had to work this hard to
be a good person. if everyone else felt this exhausted all
the time.

she looked at me like she wanted to cry

I sighed. she was a young white woman who moved
here from a quiet white town. people like her don't ask
themselves if they're good. they don't ask themselves
anything about themselves. they just go on living.

brown women, we've had to learn to be mean. to be sharp
tongue and sharper teeth. I wasn't born tough. I was soft a
long time. but I did inherit a mouth that never stops. I can
talk my way out of any room, into any heart. what to do
with this kind of power? how to keep it from going bad?
every day I wake up, I say to myself, *be good. be good. be
good.* sometimes I'm not and I think about it for weeks.

the woman is confused.

I stop trying to explain. I think of my tías and mami.
their gossip at the table as a means to survival. *be careful
with him. don't trust her, do you know that…* we are used to
having things taken from us. we turn to our words. good
words. bad words. words that say too much. I am too
much. all the time. it is a blessing. it is a curse.

the therapist nods.

A Miscarriage

s

I'm not crying
because of the dead baby

> it was going to die anyway
> either by God's will or mine

> God found it first
> saved me
> and the fetus
> from myself

I am crying because
I am supposed to happy
and I am not

everything I ever wanted
is a sleeping beast
at my feet
and I
nudge it with my toe
look it over
say, *fair enough*

what happens when I stay hungry?
when this is all I feel?

the parts
that make me,
falling out
in clots
staining the porcelain
of my tub
snaking their way
down the drain
their tail
a quick flicker
of almost
relief

what if this is it?

all the dead
babies
and enough poems
to bury myself
alive

When The Poems Don't Come

I book a room in a hotel and escape for four days / *this
will be it* / I do not write a single poem / I drink wine / I
get in the pool / I cry over frustrated love / I check out
of the hotel / get my nails done / no poems / walk in the
heat to a coffee shop / no poem / uber to my favorite book
store / a young woman approaches me / *I love your work* /
I want to sob in her arms / mourn my missing words / the
bookstore asks if I want to do a reading / I say yes / give
them dates / the book isn't written / I think of my poems
as a pen / in a purse full of what I can't find / I empty the
purse / turn my world inside out / shake it all / there's
nothing / until I call the last man who broke my heart /
hello. how are you? I miss you...

Knives
t

the story goes,
the man was not a stranger. my mother knew his name. a
machete pressed to her side. she turned teeth and nails
into her own knives and managed to get away.

the story goes,
the man was not a stranger. my mother knew his name.
a cab and his hands using her curls as a rope to pull her
where she did not want to go. my mother again used her
knives.

the story goes,
the man is my father. my mother asleep. drunk hands in
the dark. my mother says no. fists in the dark. my mother
cries herself to sleep.

the story goes,
the man is my cousin-in-law. I am six years old. his penis a
strange creature in his hands. the sky dark as my eyes.

the story goes,
the man was not a stranger. I knew his name. met him
for dinner. afterwards his car closed in around me. teeth
found my breasts. I used the knives to get away.

the story goes,
the man is a stranger. I am a girl with her drunk friend on
a bench. a gun and snarl. years of men breathing down
my neck. I know my way out. I get us home safe.

the story goes,
there is a phone call from my country. the man is my
favorite uncle. the sweetest of them all. this time a ten-
year-old. I don't know how she got away. her mother must
have given her the knives.

the story goes,
every woman has a story.

the story goes,
the men who raised us are someone else's stories.
sometimes our own.

the story goes,
a man listens to a group of girlfriends talking in a bar.
sharing stories the way folks talk about surviving a
war. long lists of close encounters. of assault. of rape.
a girlfriend sharing her location. a screen shot. just in
case. of loving the night but terrified of what it brings
out of men. loving a wolf. being the lamb. keys between
knuckles. pepper spray in pockets. a hammer in the car.
two women locking eyes in a bus full of men. leaving a
room when there are no other women. the long way home
to avoid the stranger behind you. long lists of exhaustion.
of anger. of rage.

a man listens

maybe the man is you
or your boy
or your brother
or your neighbor

the man,
hisses
not all of ussss

and we women
blink
filing our knives
knowing
we will need them
to get ourselves
home

all my poems are about love

La Novela

what if it the ending is this:

the man leaves or stays or never shows up
and the woman does not blink an eye
instead, lives a full life

the little girl watching at home
says
one day it'll be me

and it is

Soltera

one time Tía Marina chased her husband
around the lemon trees with a frying pan
after he spent all their money on alcohol

another time Tía Reina's husband
tried fighting
the other husbands
she walked outside and said to him
deja de tus chingaderas, vámonos
and he followed her home

in our family
anytime something broke
a door, a pipe, a child
the women would pull out the tools
and fix it themselves

the men somewhere else, falling apart

don't you want a husband?
a distant relative asks at a party

I sip my Hennessy and ask,
for what?

I love you

I love you. I love you. I love you. I love you. did I tell you
that the last thing I told my father was I love you? well,
the last thing I told him when he was conscious was I
love you. the last thing I told him while he was on the
respirator was *it's okay to leave, I love you.* I text you this
morning about the tv show we both love, I love you. I
text you this afternoon about the email I owe you, I love
you. I called you to tell you I was running late, I love you.
I was leaving the room, I love you. I bumped into you at
the supermarket, I love you. I thought of you at 3 pm, I
love you. if there is anything you know for certain in this
world. every day. all the time. I love you.

A Guanaca In Los Angeles

yo soy de aquí
y soy de allá

mi corazón
se viste
con las luces
de Sunset Blvd
el trafico del 101
el olor del Café Tropical
y la bulla de Los Globos

mi piel se baña
en el Río de Jalponga
La Puntilla
y la cañada que pasa
por la casa de mi abuela

estas mismas manos
parten pupusas y pizza
mis caderas bailan
cumbias y hip hop
amo a todas mis parejas
con mis dos lenguas

en ambos países
soy complicada y tierna,
la misma colocha
con labios rojos
y un amor
que no sabe
nada de fronteras

Saya

f

Tía says my eyes are two night skies and my hair dark as
the ocean at midnight. I laugh. she says funny things all
the time. she kisses my hands and says my brown skin is
the prettiest she's ever seen. makes my face feel warm and
my heart grow. Tía's job is to write stories and I help her.
we have a pretend friend named Fluffy and Fluffy always
makes a mess. Tía says everyone is messy sometimes.
when it's cold we sit on her big chair and share a blanket.
I tell her I want to watch bidi bidi bom bom. did you
know that Selena looks like me? brown hair and eyes.
when Tía cries I pretend not to notice. I know it's because
she loves me a lot and sometimes it doesn't fit inside her
and leaks out through the eyes. she's going to write a book
about me one day. *you're crazy!* I tell her. we sing bidi bidi
bom bom really loud until Abuela says she can't hear her
novela. we laugh. Tía is crying again.

La Tía

r

my two-year-old nephew
laughs when I
press my mouth to his belly

if I say *besito*
he pulls my face
close to his
and covers me with kisses

when I enter the room
he squeals with joy
flings his arms around his sister
and they tumble to the ground
howling my name

I don't know motherhood
but I know this;
two tiny bodies
I'd let the skies
crush me for

Ode To A Fat Girl's Crop Top

sweet shirt
made of little fabric
folded and unfolded
tucked into the bottom drawer
pulled out and inspected
worn in hesitance
exposing one single strip
of tender flesh
anxious hands tugging at your hem
mothers and aunts asking
where the rest of you has gone
ay mija, why can't you wear a regular shirt?
se te mira toda la panza.

out in the world you become
a fuck you
a fist ready to fight
a *go ahead and look as long as you want*
a strut down a crosswalk
a laugh at turned up noses
an *I don't give a shit, I look damn good*

a parade
a victory
a graduation, wedding and quinceañera
happening at the same damn time

a fat girl who loved herself today

Oakland

u

a man and I
press together in a hotel lobby
I ask him
what his favorite part
on a woman's body is
and he answers
the clitoris
designed
for nothing
but pleasure
I laugh
he laughs
we kiss
he bites my lip
I close my eyes
an elevator dings
out pours a group of people
we all exchange knowing glances
they trail whispers and giggles
I do not care
I pull him in for another kiss
the moon is full
and I have a meal to feed him

Hollywood

the three of us sat in a restaurant in Hollywood. hair,
lipstick and nails type of women. spoke about our careers,
plans, men, homegirls, goals. ate and laughed. punctuating
each sentence with hand gestures. hair flips at the end
of dramatic stories. plates full of good food, mouths full
of good chisme. at the table next to us a family. mom,
dad, brother and little sister. the sister a quiet brown
girl with big eyes. her family staring at their phones the
entire meal. she and I made eye contact. I smiled. she
smiled and never looked away. my friends and I continued
talking, eating and drinking. we closed our bill, gathered
our purses, headed out the door. the little girl followed us
with her eyes. I winked. soon she will also be an electric
current in a room. flash of dark hair, teeth framed by bold
lips. she will think of the women in Hollywood. she too,
will never compromise. will make other little girls stare in
awe. they too, in turn, become electric and free.

Endulzar

I need to finish this poem

don't
he says
pulls me back into bed
bites my bottom lip and laughs

I let my hands
do what hands
like to do with bodies

the poem
is written in
red
across
his back

10:15pm

i

what are you wearing? I text her. it's Friday and there's a
dance floor waiting for our heels. in the bathroom I play
my music loud while I shower. a dress rehearsal. minutes
later I lean into the mirror. my lips turned blood red
or midnight black. bruja colors. my gold hoop earrings
reflect the light, their own dance. on comes the good
bra. the sheer cropped top. up come the jeans too tight
to walk in until I do a couple of squats to stretch them.
I lean over the bathroom sink. my hair a curtain around
me. my fingers tugging the roots. the bigger the hair, the
more boys it catches. I find my perfume, spray it into my
curls. something sweet for a dance partner to find when
his lips graze my neck. *I'm ready.* I text her. I look at myself
one last time. all my thirty-four years framed in the mirror,
artwork.

At My Funeral

t

at my funeral
I want you to play bidi bidi bom bom
followed by back that ass up
followed by Juan Gabriel
followed by Drake

at my funeral
I want you to eat all you can
please don't turn down my mami's food
she will be grieving and offer you platefuls
say yes to each one
this will make her feel closer to me

at my funeral
don't read any of my poems
I wrote those to stay alive
let them rest
stretch their limbs
pack their bags
find new fingers

at my funeral
let the men make jokes
I have understood that
masculinity only allows them
to be tender through laughter
I want them soft and sweet
during my final goodbye

at my funeral
thank the women
my mother
my sisters

my girlfriends
kiss their palms
keep their tissues
they are holy
and what I am
saddest about leaving

at my funeral
let the babies run free
kiss their heads
sneak pastries into
their chubby hands
watch their faces flush
with delight

at my funeral
find the little girls
and let them
try on my lipsticks
especially the red ones
let them walk through
the house
each mouth
a rose bud
made for me

at my funeral
don't feel obligated to cry
dance if that's what your body asks
remember mine
felt most alive
beneath strobe lights
and loud music

I will be dead,
of course,

and this will be a victory

praise the sudden illness
or accident that claimed me
praise the hospital bed
I exhaled in
praise the doctors
and nurses
and prayers
that tried to keep me

praise this heart of mine
that couldn't anymore
praise all the years that came
wrapped themselves
around my legs
and pulled me away

praise my death
because it did not come
from my own hands
from razor blade
or pill

instead because
it was time
because my body
or my God
said
come home
and I collected everything
that I am and
walked through that door

at my funeral
play a song

that says
I survived myself

praised be such a
sweet
sweet
end

este libro fue posible gracias a las mujeres de la familia
Palacios
mi mami, mamita, tías, primas y hermanas.
mi gran trabajo en esta vida es celebrar las a ustedes
todo lo que soy es por todo lo que ustedes han
sobrevivido.

special thank you to my home
Da Poetry Lounge
and the unyielding love it continues to give me

my heart also belongs to communities of
Chingona Fire
Espacio 1839 in Boyle Heights
Grand Studio in Oakland

my final prayer of gratitude is for
all the women who hold me close to the sun
my chillonas and desmadrosas

may we always be too much

About the Author

Yesika Salgado is a Los Angeles based Salvadoran poet who writes about her family, her culture, her city and her brown body. She has shared her work in venues and campuses throughout the country. Salgado is a four time member of Da Poetry Lounge Slam Team and a 2017 and 2018 National Poetry Slam finalist. Her work has been featured in *Latina Magazine, Univision, Vibe Magazine, Huffington Post, NPR, TEDx* and many other digital platforms. She is the Co-founder of the Latina feminist collective Chingona Fire and an internationally recognized body positivity activist. Yesika is the author of the Amazon best-seller *Corazón* and her newest collection of poetry *Tesoro*, both published with Not A Cult.